Type and Text Faster

Time-Saving Tips to Communicate More
Efficiently

Robert Moutal

Medialusion Group

Contents

About This Book

There is nothing worse than reading long books with only a few pages of quality information, and the rest is just fluff. This book is packed with actionable information that will save you hours of time, right away!

My goal is to help you change the way you think about repetitive tasks, and stop typing the same words and phrases over and over again.

In this book, you'll learn how to use text expanders in various ways.

This lead-by-example guide will teach you everything you need to know about using text expanders - at work, home, on your computer or smartphone. You'll be surprised at how easy and powerful it is!

Introduction

I'm just gonna come out and say it:

My name is Robert Moutal and I am a lazy person.

Give me any complex task and I will look for ways to do it well, but with the least effort, and in the shortest possible amount of time.

I'm also a tech geek! If you show me a shiny new object, I'll be distracted for hours!

I have been using text expanders for years to boost my productivity.

As a 16-Emmy Award winning TV producer, I had to write scripts for commercials, news pieces, and sketches. Then, as the General Manager, I wrote thousands of emails to clients, vendors, employees, and management.

After that, I founded my own company, and I had to write sales letters, email sequences, brochures, website content...

Oh my God, so much writing!

Since I spend most of my day writing and texting, I needed a way to make my work more efficient.

And that's where text expanders came to the rescue, helping me save over 17 hours every month!

17 hours?... that can't be true! Right? (the proof is at the end of Chapter 1)

But, let me leave you with a little taste:

I write at least 35 emails a day, and each one begins with "I hope all is well with you."

I spend 4.24 minutes a day typing that simple line alone. In a month, that's 127 minutes, or 2.12 hours. Calculate that, and you'll come up with 25.1 hours a year!

Don't use a text expander, and you'll just spend a whole day of your life typing *"I hope you're doing well."*

Do I have your attention now? Read on...

1

Text Expanders

What Are Text Expanders and Why Should You Use Them?

A text expander is an extension for text editors that helps you write faster by reducing the time you spend typing repetitive words, phrases, and sentences.

It's even possible to write complete paragraphs with a few keystrokes!

The system automatically expands short abbreviations into full text after you type them.

For writers having to deal with a lot of repetition in their writing, text expanders can be a great time-saving tool.

If you want to know why you should use a text expander, consider these examples:

Example #1:

In Chapter 4, you'll find a list of "100 things you type over and over again, but didn't even realize you did". There are about 3,600 characters, of which most are shortened to between 3 and 4 characters.

It is estimated that the average typing speed of a person is about 40 words per minute (WPM) or 190 characters per minute (CPM).

Typing all 3,600 characters would take an average person 19 minutes, while typing just the 400 characters of the combined 100 shortcuts would only take around 2 minutes.

In other words, just this list alone will save you 17 minutes of your time, which doesn't sound like much... yet.

Keep reading...

Example #2

Imagine how much you could save if instead of simply expanding *"tyvm"* to a simple phrase like *"Thank you very much"*, you expanded a shortcut like *"linkedintro"* (11 characters) into a full 900 character introductory message to send to 100 potential clients on LinkedIn.

Here's the math for that one:

- 11-character shortcut X 100 = 1100 characters typed.

- At 190 CPM, this equals 5.78 minutes of actual typing

Compare that to:

- A 900-character LinkedIn introduction X 100 = 90,000 characters.

- At 190 CPM, this would equal 473 minutes or 7.89 hours saved!

You could argue that you could simply copy and paste the text from a Word document into different LinkedIn profiles every time. Yes, you absolutely could.

But, remember that you might also have to copy/paste the recipient's name into each message, then return to your word document and copy the entire 900-character message!

There is so much work involved in that!

Example #3:

The following 8 phrases are part of pretty much every email I write every day. On a slow day, I write about 35 emails that include all 8 phrases.

In (parentheses) I'm including the shortcuts I created, which trigger each phrase.

"I hope all is well with you." (**welll**)

"Please let me know if you need anything else." (**lll**)

"Thank you, and have a great day." (**t0**)

"Best regards," (**br,**)

"Robert Moutal (**titeng**)
Co-Founder,
Clarity Wave
claritywave.com"

"4400 Calle Mar de Armonia" (**4400**)

"San Diego" (**sdie**)

"858-449-4100 (**ttel**)

These phrases have a total of **224 characters,** whereas their shortcuts only have **31**.

Check out the math below.

Phrase	Chars.	Shortcut	Actually saved	Emails in a day	Total characters saved	CPM	Minutes saved per day	Minutes saved per month	Hours saved per month	Hours saved per year
Thank you, and have a great day.	32	2	30	35	1050	190	5.53	165.79	2.76	33.2
I hope all is well with you.	28	5	23	35	805	190	4.24	127.11	2.12	25.4
Best regards,	13	3	10	35	350	190	1.84	55.26	0.92	11.1
Please let me know if you need anything else.	45	3	42	35	1470	190	7.74	232.11	3.87	46.4
rmoutal@claritywave.com	5	3	2	35	70	190	0.37	11.05	0.18	2.2
Robert Moutal Co-Founder, Clarity Wave claritywave.com	55	3	52	35	1820	190	9.58	287.37	4.79	57.5
4488 Calle Mar de Armonia	25	4	21	35	735	190	3.87	116.05	1.93	23.2
San Diego	9	4	5	35	175	190	0.92	27.63	0.46	5.5
858-449-4106	12	4	8	35	280	190	1.47	44.21	0.74	8.8
TOTAL							35.55	1066.58	17.78	213.3

Every month, I save more than 17 hours.

213.3 hours each year! That's almost 9 full days of my life!

Is This For Me?

But what if you're not a writer or a marketer?

You may think you have to be a full-time writer or novelist to take advantage of text expanders, but that's not the case.

In a typical day, how many emails do you send or receive?

Do you ever find yourself typing the same sentence or word over and over again?

I'm not talking about writing a sentence 1,000 times obsessively, like Bart Simpson.

In Chapter 4, I will show you 100 sentences that could save you hours of your time.

What about text messaging on your phone? The average person sends 72 text messages each day.

Do you want to save those thumbs some pain and be quick on your hands?

As soon as you discover the true potential of text expanders, you will wonder how on Earth you ever managed without them!

Use Cases

It's time to change the way you think about writing. Here are some ideas of how to use text expanders in everyday life.

Use Case #1 -

Fill out recurring email snippets automatically

Snippets are a useful feature of most text expanders if you spend all your time sending emails.

These are blocks of text that can be accessed with just a few keystrokes. In other words, you can save the text of your first email as a snippet and reuse it in subsequent emails asking your client to pay your invoice instead of typing a new message every time.

The advantage of this method of saving text is that it is more modular than, say, a full email template.

As a result, you can divide recurring emails into parts and add different elements as you see fit.

Use Case #2 -

Depending on who you're contacting, customize your email signature

You can use email signatures to provide people with information about yourself, without making your emails too long.

Perhaps you prefer a more professional-looking signature for coworkers than your friends, or you want different information for clients than colleagues.

It's easy to tailor your emails by creating different signatures and assigning them to different abbreviations (like "sig1" or "sig2").

Use Case #3 -

On-the-fly calculation of due dates and other important data

You can, for instance, automatically enter certain data into your snippets with the help of intelligent macro editing.

Suppose you want to send someone an email telling them that payment is due in two weeks.

Use math macros to automatically add 14 days to the current date when you use the snippet, instead of pulling up your calendar.

The calculator will not only save you time, but also do the math for you.

Math is easy for computers!

Let them handle it!

Use Case #4 -

Fix common mistakes (that autocorrect doesn't catch) automatically

You might get that little red squiggle under things like proper nouns and proprietary words when you misspell something.

Adding the name of your boss, *Mr. Hoffstetter*, to your text expander will ensure you never accidentally misspell his name if you accidentally type something else.

When working with others, text expanders are better than auto correct, because they allow you to share snippets with your team (see next use case):

Use Case #5 -

Get your team members to share your snippets

The shortcuts you create can be shared and synchronized with everyone on a team (though teams are often a paid feature), so not only can you avoid spelling your boss's name incorrectly, but you can make sure nobody else does as well.

Use Case #6 -

Lorem ipsum

If you're a graphic designer or web developer, or anyone who uses simulated placeholder text regularly, having a shortcut that expands to the familiar Lorem ipsum block of text is a huge time saver.

If you don't know what that is, here's an example:

Lorem ipsum dolor sit amet, consectetur adipiscing elit, sed do eiusmod tempor incididunt ut labore et dolore magna aliqua. Ut enim ad minim veniam, quis nostrud exercitation ullamco laboris nisi ut aliquip ex ea commodo consequat.

Duis aute irure dolor in reprehenderit in voluptate velit esse cillum dolore eu fugiat nulla pariatur. Excepteur sint occaecat cupidatat non proident, sunt in culpa qui officia deserunt mollit anim id est laborum.

Use Case #7 -

Templates

Having a shortcut for regularly used templates is a huge time saver.

For example, if you like to journal every day, you might want to create a template with the questions you ask yourself daily, like:

1. What did I enjoy?

2. What did I learn?

3. Was I better today than yesterday?

4. How can I do things better tomorrow?

5. What is my attention focused on right now?

6. What am I grateful for today?

Use Case #8 -

Words with apostrophes

Sometimes, when I write words with apostrophes, like "doesn't", "isn't", "didn't", "you're", etc. I accidentally hit "Return/Enter" instead of the apostrophe, since they're right next to each other.

That's usually a problem when I'm chatting, because "Enter" usually sends the message immediately, and that can be awkward at times.

So, I created a list of all the words that use apostrophes and autocorrect them with my text expansion app.

Now, I simply type *"isnt"* or *"dont"* and the text expander takes care of the rest!

Use Case #9 -

Special Symbols

When you're trying to remember the special key combination of certain symbols, like £, €, ®, °, etc., an easy-to-remember shortcut can save you a lot of time.

For example:

"gbp" expands to £

"degreees" expands to °

"eeuro" expands to €

Yes, you're actually typing more characters than you're expanding, but you're also saving time looking for the key combinations.

4

Useful Tips

When creating a shortcut, here are a few useful tips:

3 letters in a row

I like to use three letters in a row. For example: ppp, jjj, vvv.

PROS:

Three letters in a row are not common in regular English writing, and they are incredibly quick to type.

Three letters are easy to remember, especially when they correspond to the first letter of the key word or sentence you're trying to expand (e.g. "qqq" expands to "*Thank you for your question.*"

CONS:

There are only 26 lowercase letters in the alphabet.

Combining upper and lower cases would double, triple, or even quadruple the possibilities, but it would be much harder to remember.

PRO TIP: Avoid using "aaa" (which, in the US is the name of the roadside assistance service / insurance company) or "www" which you might still use when typing in a web address.

Examples:

- "qqq" expands to "*Thank you for your question*"

- "ppp" expands to "*Password*"

- "lll" expands to "*Please let me know if you need anything else.*"

- "ooo" expands to "*Please let me know if you have any other questions.*
  Best regards,
  Robert"

  (Yes, you can expand to full paragraphs with line breaks and all the works)

- "ttt" expands to "*Perfect. Thank you.*"

- "fff" expands to "*I'm looking forward to talking to you soon.*"

Words with extra letters at the beginning, middle or end

Adding an extra letter at the beginning, middle or end of a normal word is something that doesn't happen naturally when typing, and it makes it super easy to remember what you're trying to replace.

Examples:

- **"welll"** (end) expands to "*I hope all is well with you.*"

- **"ttel"** (beginning) expands to your phone number

- **"linkk"** (end) expands to a link you need to use regularly

- **"maill"** (end) expands to your email address

- **"bumpp"** (end) expands to *"I just want to bump this back up in your inbox."*

- **"zooom"** (middle) expands to your Zoom link

Words with combinations of letters and numbers

Adding a number to a word allows you to expand to words or phrases in the same category.

Examples:

Email addresses

- **"mail1"** expands to your personal email

- **"mail2"** expands to your business email

Salutations

- **"welll"** expands to *"I hope all is well with you."*

- **"well1"** expands to *"I hope you had a great weekend"*.

- **"well2"** expands to *"I hope you're having a great week, so far."*

Thank you's

- **"t0"** expands to *"Thank you, and have a great day."*

- **"t1"** expands to *"Thank you, and have a great weekend."*

- **"t2"** expands to *"Thank you, and have a great evening."*

-

"**t4**" expands to "*Thank you, and have a great rest of your week.*"

Links

- "**calend60**" expands to a link to a 60-minute Calendly meeting

- "**calend30**" expands to a link to a 30-minute Calendly meeting

- "**calend15**" expands to a link to a 15-minute Calendly meeting

Shortcuts with double syllables or double alternating letters

My favorite shortcuts are these, because they are very easy to remember. Just type two or three letters twice.

Examples:

- "**pwpw**" expands to a very complex password

- "**refref**" expands to "*Thank you for referring me to* "

- **"sdsd"** expands to *"San Diego"*

- **"nyny"** expands to *"New York"*

- **"lili"** expands to a full LinkedIn connection request message I type over and over

Acronyms and initialisms

These are commonly used when texting, and can also be expanded to full phrases.

And, when you think about it, people use these abbreviations because they don't want to type the whole phrase. So now, with a text expander, you can still use the abbreviation and look good doing it!

Examples:

- **"tyvm"** expands to *"Thank you very much."*

- **"brb"** expands to *"I'll be right back"*

- **"lol"** expands to *"That's hilarious"* (who said you need to expand it to "laughing out loud"?)

- **"imo"** expands to *"In my opinion"*

- "**ooh**" expands to "*On one hand,*"

- "**otoh**" expands to "*on the other hand*"

- "**btw**" expands to "*by the way*"

- "**omw**" expands to "*On my way!*"**

** If you have your mobile phone handy, pull it out right now and type "omw" on any text field (i.e. email, text, chat).

Did it give you the option to select "On my way!"? That's because iPhones and some Android devices already have that shortcut preset for you.

See? You just expanded your first phrase! :-)

Using special characters for different types of shortcuts

Creating shortcuts that begin with a particular character, for example ";" or "/" allows you to create shortcuts using very few letters, while simultaneously categorizing them.

Examples:

- Use ";" for all your links:

- ○ **;v1** expands to link of video A

- ○ **;v2** expands to link of video B

- Use "/" for different website addresses

  - ○ **/p** expands to the pricing page link on your website

  - ○ **/f** expands to the features page link on your website

5

Pro Tips

Y ou've mastered the essentials. Now, these pro tips will take your text expanding to new levels!

Make shortcuts based on your immediate needs.

Make a temporary shortcut if you plan to type something more than five times, which you can delete once you're done.

- **"yryr"** expands to "*Happy New Year! I hope 2023 brings you all the joy in the world*".

- **"xcxc"** expands to *"expands to ""*.

If you noticed, I used *"expands to ""* a lot throughout this document. So why not create a shortcut? Note I even added the opening quotation sign.

BONUS TIP:

When creating ad-hoc shortcuts, it's better to use two letters next to each other on the keyboard, even if they don't make sense, rather than two letters far apart. For example, "**xcxc**" is easier to type than "**exex**", which would make more sense for the phrase I was trying to abbreviate (expands to).

In the end, this shortcut will only be used once and then deleted

Include spaces or special characters, such as quotation marks or open parenthesis, on your expanded text.

If you're expanding a sentence followed by more words (i.e. not a full sentence), why not include the space after it in the shortcut? This way, you don't need to type it.

Example: "**meetmeet**" expands to *"I'm looking forward to talking to you on[space]"* (because that phrase would be followed by a date and time).

In the previous Pro Tip, "**xcxc**" expanded to *expands to"*, which included the quotation mark.

Be mindful of shortcuts that might accidentally be part of other words

If a shortcut accidentally expands when you're typing a word that includes it, use all caps instead.

For example, even though the short **"ugh"** doesn't seem to make much sense, think of all the words that would trigger it: Tough, enough, rough, etc.

Be careful of accidental trailing spaces

When creating a shortcut, be careful not to include a trailing space inadvertently. Such a trailing space is not readily discernible and can be missed, meaning that your abbreviation will not expand as expected unless you include the space when typing it.

For example:

- "**ggg**" (correct)

- "**ggg** " (incorrect)

What about capitalization for phrases that can appear at the beginning or the middle of a sentence?

Do you need to create different shortcuts for things like: "*To be honest*" (starting a sentence) and "*to be honest*" (in the middle of one)?

The answer is: Depends.

Some extensions allow you to automatically adapt the content to the case of the shortcut. So, "**Tbh**" would capitalize "*To*" and "**tbh**" would not.

6

100 common things you didn't even realize you typed over and over

Every day, you type or text at least one or two of the items on the following list.

Here are some of the most commonly used phrases and expressions people type over and over. Come up with a shortcut that makes the most sense to you, using some of the tips from earlier.

However, there are a few universally accepted abbreviations used in texting that you might also want to include as text expanders.

1. Your name

2. Your title

3. Your email signature

4. Your address

5. Your email address

6. Your phone number

7. Your credit card number

8. Your CCV code

9. Your city

10. Your company website

11. Your bank routing number

12. Your bank account number (use with caution)

13. Your company tax ID number (use with caution)

14. I'm not interested at the moment. Thank you. (Great for unsolicited messages)

15. Thank you very much.

16. Thank you, and have a great day.

17. Thank you, and have a great weekend.

18. Thank you, and have a great evening.

19. Thank you, and give my best to (space).

20. I hope all is well with you.

21. I hope you had a great weekend.

22. I hope you had a great holiday.

23. I hope you had a great long weekend.

24. I hope you feel better soon.

25. I hope you enjoyed your vacation.

26. Happy birthday. I hope you have a great one! (Great for Facebook birthday messages)

27. Best regards, (your name)

28. Your company name

29. I'm looking forward to (talking, meeting, seeing you, working with you, etc.)

30. Thank you for your reply

31. Thank you for your feedback

32. Thank you for your email.

33. Thank you for reaching out.

34. Thank you for getting back to me.

35. Thank you for letting me know.

36. Just a friendly reminder that (space)

37. Could you please (space)

38. I would love to (space)

39. I'd be happy to (space)

40. I am writing to you about (space)

41. I'm reaching out because (space)

42. Please let me know if you have any questions.

43. Do not hesitate to (space)

44. Please let me know if you need anything else.

45. Awesome! Thank you.

46. Perfect. Thank you.

47. I agree with you.

48. Please confirm receipt.

49. Attached please find (space)

50. Best regards,

51. Warmest regards,

52. Best wishes

53. All the best,

54. Let me do some research and get back to you

55. This is my Zoom link: (link)

56. This is a link to my calendar availability: (link)

57. Please give me a call at (number)

58. I would like to (space)

59. I'm contacting you because (space)

60. I'm reaching out to (space)

61. It's been a while since we (space)

62. Are you still interested in (space)

63. Directions to find your home or business

64. Great to virtually meet you.

65. Hi, I'm (your name), (your title) of (your company name). (Elevator pitch)

66. Would you be interested in (connecting, finding out more, learning more)?

67. Thank you for your interest.

68. A common response to your customers' questions

69. Do you have a few minutes (this week, next week, today) to discuss?

70. Are you available some time (next week, this month)?

71. Great chatting with you earlier.

72. For more information, please visit (your website)

73. **icymi** expands to "In case you missed it"

74. **tbh** expands to "To be honest"

75. **lmk** expands to "let me know"

76. **idk** expands to "I don't know"

77. **eod** expands to "End of day"

78. **ooo** expands to "out of the office"

79. **tia** expands to "Thanks in advance"

80. **btw** expands to "by the way," (Include the comma when setting this one up).

81. **tmrw** expands to "tomorrow"

82. **wfm** expands to "works for me"

83. **fwiw** expands to "For what it's worth"

84. **hth** expands to "I hope this helps"

85. **iow** expands to "In other words"

86. **dgmw** expands to "Don't get me wrong"

87. **nntr** expands to "No need to reply' (*see bonus tip below)

88. **nrn** expands to "No reply necessary" (a different version of nntr)

89. **thx** expands to "Thank you"

90. **ymmd** expands to "You made my day"

91. **p2p** expands to "peer-to-peer" (any expression with

hyphens after each word is a great candidate for text expansion, as hyphens are not as quick to type as regular spaces).

92. **d2d** expands to "day-to-day"

93. **bk2bk** expands to "back-to-back" (note I didn't use b2b because that could be used to expand to business-to-business).

94. **upd** expands to "up-to-date"

95. **4yo** expands to "four-year-old" (or any number)

96. **mof** expands to "matter-of-fact"

97. **n4p** expands to "not-for-profit"

98. **nEs** expands to "non-English-speaker"

99. **MIL** expands to "mother-in-law" (also applies to FIL, SIL, BIL)

100. **YE** expands to "year-end" (notice I'm using all caps to avoid accidentally expanding words like "year" or "employee"

7

Bonus Time-Saving Tip – NRN and NNTR

Despite the fact that this tip isn't about text expansion, you'll save a lot of time and frustration with it.

It's something I use all the time.

How annoying is it when you send an email to someone only to receive a reply simply saying "Thank you"?

It is our human nature to be polite and to mind our manners.

An acknowledgement of a read email does nothing to advance the conversation, and wastes both the sender and the recipient's time, because they must now open the email, read it, and process it (archive or delete).

The NRN or NNTR allows the recipient to safely ignore politeness altogether.

My first message always includes the abbreviation as well as its meaning, since not everyone knows what NRN or NNTR means.

For example:

Dear John,

Attached please find the document you requested.
Please let me know if you need anything else.

Best regards,

Robert

NRN (No Reply Necessary) / NNTR (No Need to Reply)

8

How to Become a Text Expanding Ninja

As with any skill, improving productivity through text expansion takes time and effort.

This chapter includes a few tips for boosting your productivity without going crazy.

Start slow

Add shortcuts one at a time, rather than all at once.

You can start by adding the shortcuts you use most often, then as you discover the timesaving benefits of text expansion, add more shortcuts.

Start with your full name, which you use every day, or your address, which combines letters and numbers and is typically difficult to enter on mobile devices.

Keep shortcuts consistent

The shortcuts on your desktop and mobile devices should be the same.

Otherwise, you'll get very confused, very quickly.

Start noticing patterns

Be on the lookout for repetitive behaviors.

Think about adding a shortcut whenever you notice you type something more than five times.

This will become second nature for you in no time.

Use disposable shortcuts

Some shortcuts aren't meant to last forever.

It is possible to create shortcuts with a specific purpose in mind for a limited period.

At the end of every year, I create a list of shortcuts I'll use for a few days, and then delete them.

- Happy 2023!

- Happy New Year!

- Merry Christmas!

- Happy holidays!

- I hope your 2023 brings you lots of

- good surprises.

Review your shortcuts regularly

Open your list of shortcuts every few months, and ask yourself these questions:

Do I still use this shortcut?

Would it be possible to repurpose this shortcut to trigger a different expansion instead? (Removing shortcuts that are unused).

Keep tidy with folders

Depending on the app you use, you can also organize snippets into folders.

This makes them easier to find and edit when needed down the road.

Every person's needs are different, but we recommend at least starting with folders based on the type or purpose of your snippets.

Folders for 'Work,' 'Links,' and 'Email Responses' would be a good start.

Bonus points if you've started a 'Personal Typos' group.

Use a text expander to correct double capitalization

Sometimes I type so fast I don't release the Shift key before hitting the second letter of a word.

With most apps, you should be able to set it up so double capitals are automatically corrected.

Use a text expander for cumbersome words

There are some words that are simply too hard for me to type. For example, "*acknowledgement*" is one of those words that slow me down every time.

And I use it often, in different forms, e.g. *acknowledge, acknowledged, acknowledgement*, etc.

So, here's what I do in these cases:

1. Think of the minimum expression of the word. For example, "acknowledge" is the shortest version of the word.

2. Then create a shortcut using any of the tips above. In this case, I'm using "**ackk**".

3. Depending on the usage, I can simply add a "*d*" to make it acknowledged or a "*ment*" to make it acknowledgement.

What if you don't want to trigger the expansion?

Most apps allow you to set up a combination of keystrokes to stop it from expanding text.

For example, while writing this book, I used many of my own shortcuts as examples, and didn't want the app to constantly trigger them.

In my case, using aText, I can use Shift+Option+A to temporarily disable it.

Using text expanders for images and even attachments.

Many text expander apps allow you to include rich text, which means you can create nicely formatted snippets or even full documents.

A great use of the image expansion functionality is the creation of email signatures.

Why just have your name, title, and position, when you can also include your company logo?

Super ultra ninja tip - Using variables with your expansions.

This tip will blow your mind!

It's a little more advanced, but once you learn what it does, it will take your productivity to the next level.

Let's say you want to create a long snippet of text, like a canned email reply or a connection request, but you also want to personalize it.

Some more advanced apps, like TextExpander and aText, allow you to insert variables, which you can then fill in before inserting.

To better illustrate this, I'll give you first what I was doing before learning this trick:

BEFORE:

I wrote a LinkedIn connection request text that read, more or less like this:

"Hi (space),

Thank you for connecting with me.

I love what you're doing at (space).

Let's discuss more ways in which we can (space)

I'm looking forward to chatting with you soon.

Robert"

This meant that every time I expanded this text, I'd have to manually move my mouse over each location where I left a space, and fill in the information.

But what if I don't want to type in all that missing information? Well, that's where variables come in.

AFTER:

*"Hi **[name field, with "there" as default text]**,*

Thank you for connecting with me.

*I love what you're doing at **[company field, with***

***"your company" as default text]**.*

Let's discuss more ways in which we can [text

field, with no default]

I'm looking forward to chatting with you soon.

Robert"

As a result, when I trigger the expansion, the app opens a window where I can fill in the missing fields, or leave them blank to display a default text.

There is also a function in TextExpander (I haven't seen it on aText) that allows you to turn off or on complete sections or paragraphs.

Doing this, you can create one shortcut with multiple expansion options, for example, an email with multiple responses based on the type of email.

9

Text Expansion on Your Mobile Device

If most of your typing is done on your mobile device, then text expansion should definitely help your thumbs in the long run.

In both iOS and Android devices, you can create text replacement shortcuts that, when triggered, show as suggestions as you type.

iOS

This is the process to create shortcuts on iPhone and iPad devices:

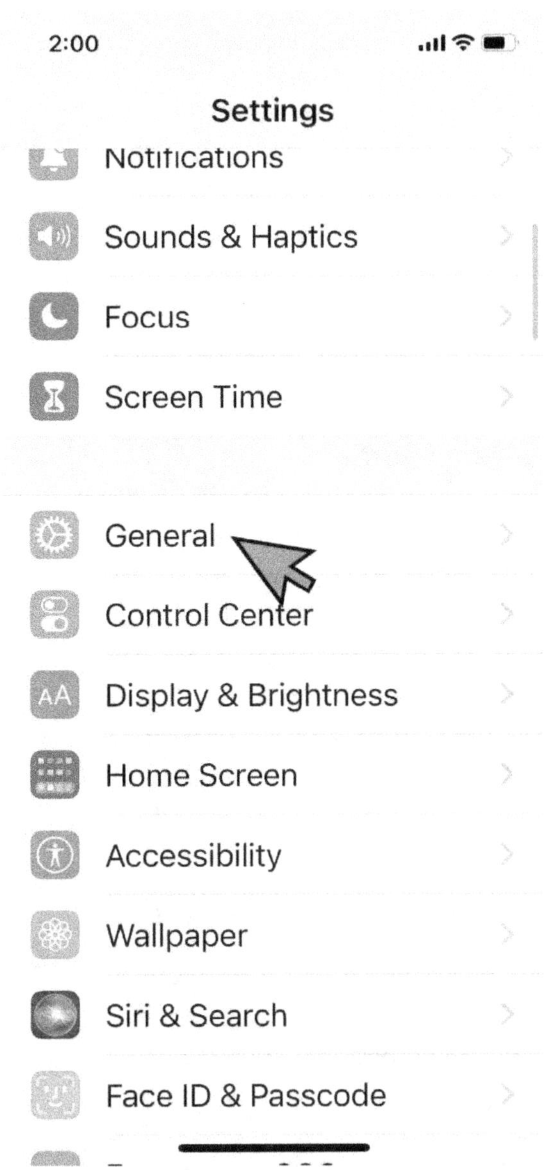

Go to Settings and then General

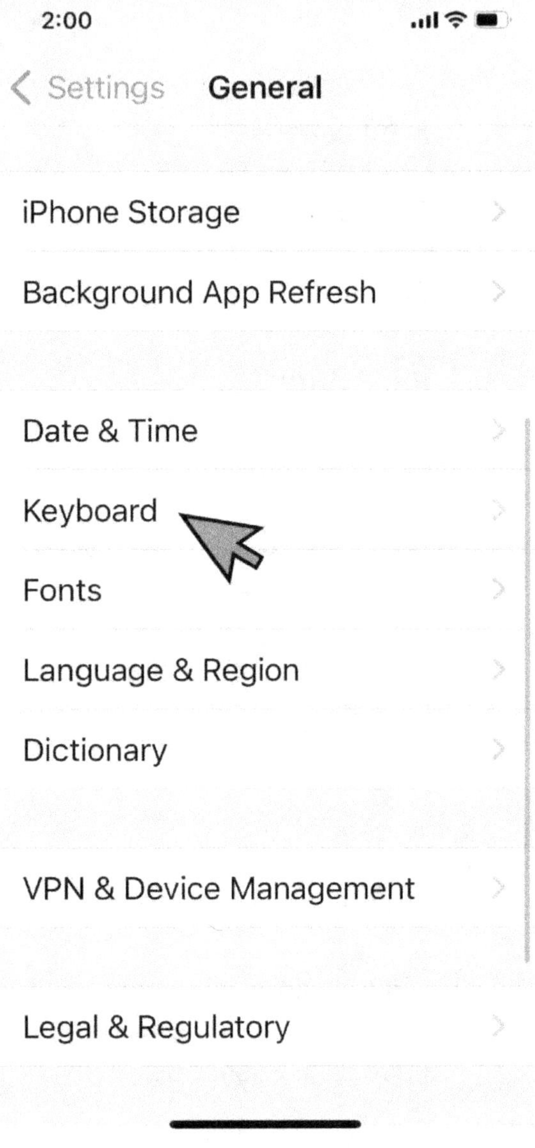

Tap on Keyboard

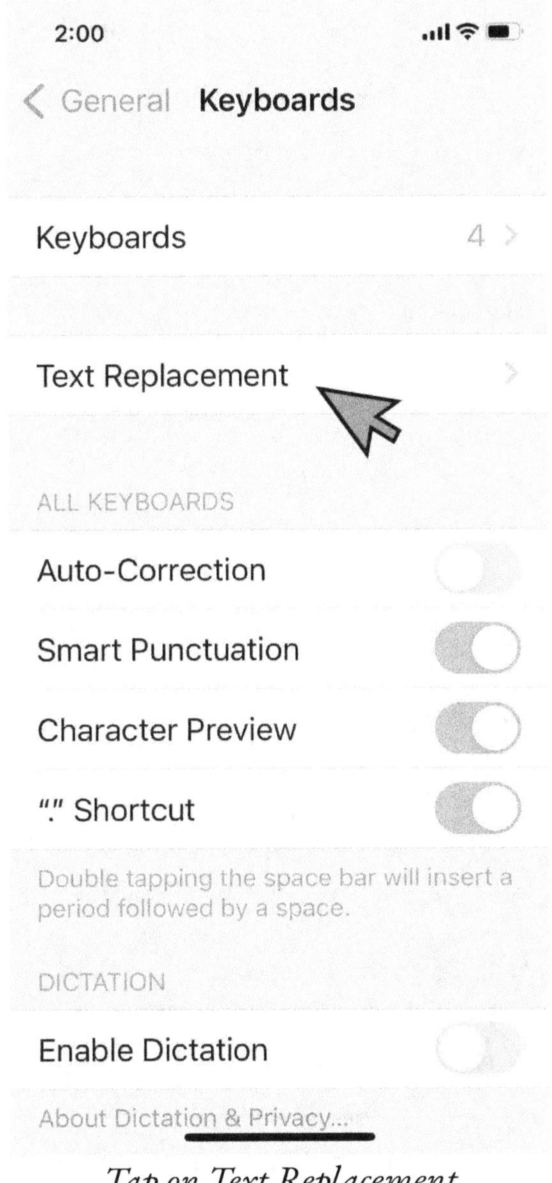

Tap on Text Replacement

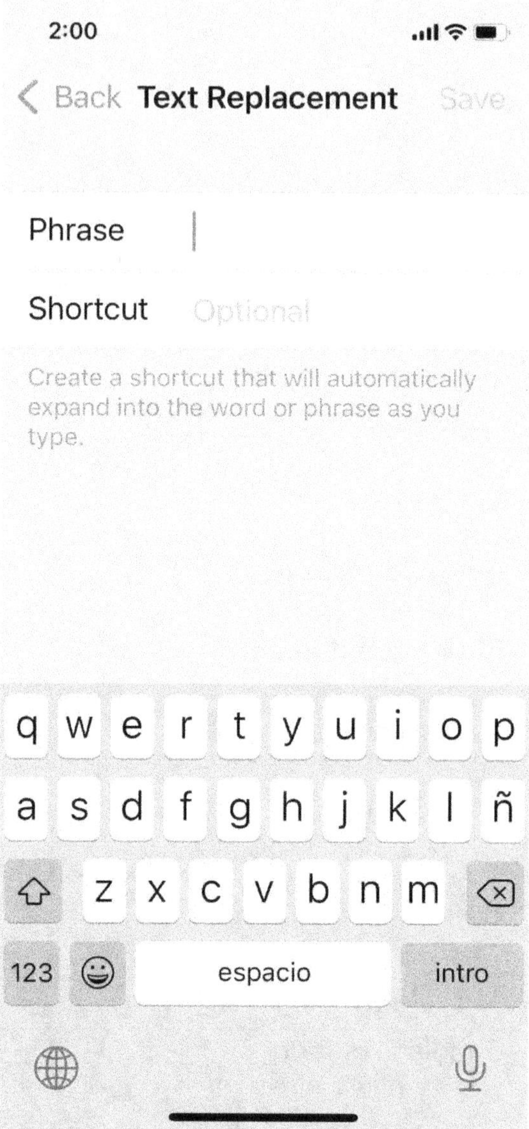

Type in your Phrase and Shortcut

Android

This is the process to create shortcuts on Android devices.

(Instructions may differ for different devices, these are for Samsung

phones).

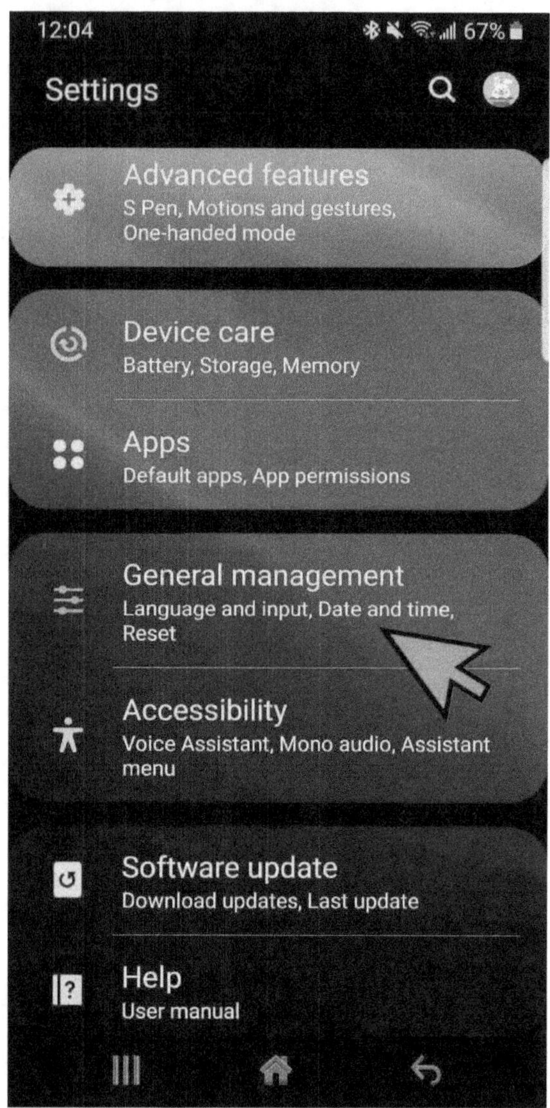

Go to Settings and then General Management

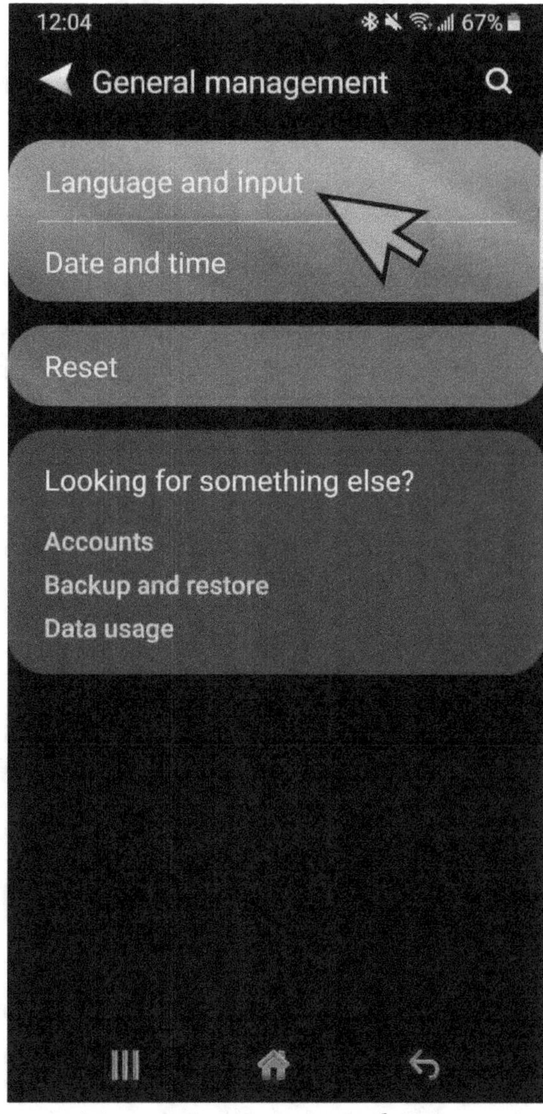

Tap on Language and Input

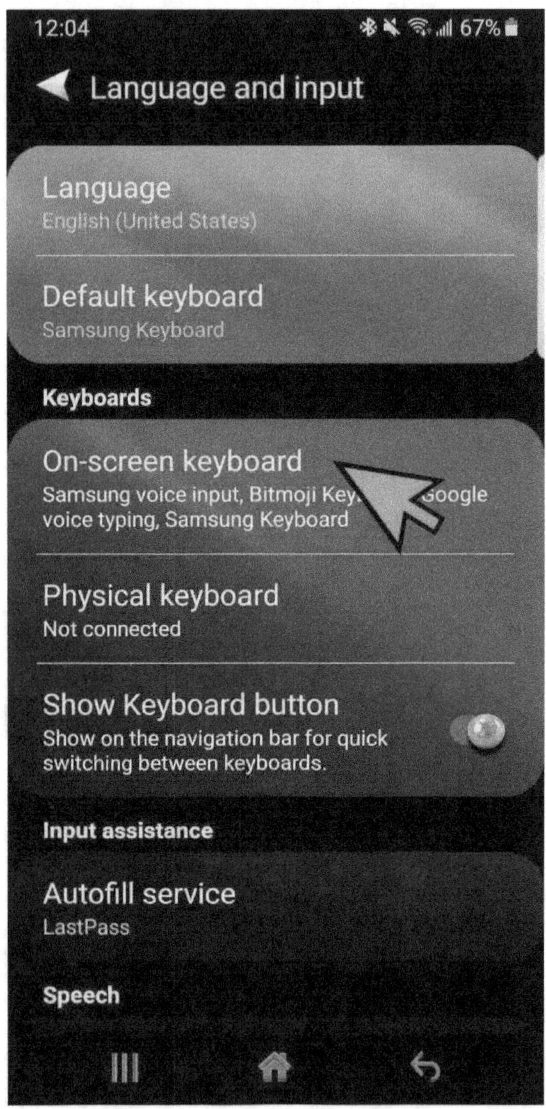

Tap on On-screen Keyboard

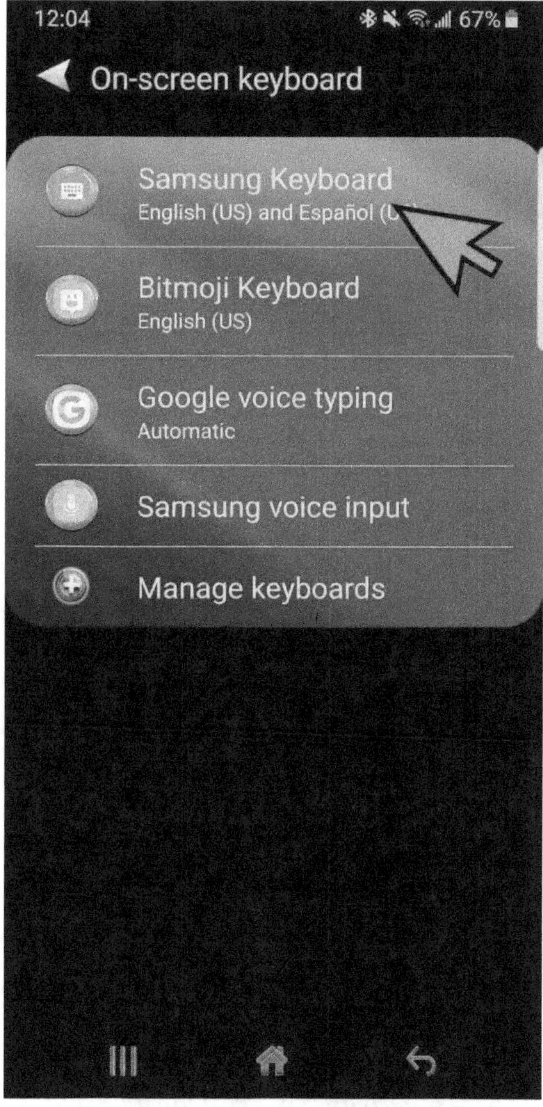

Select the Samsung Keyboard

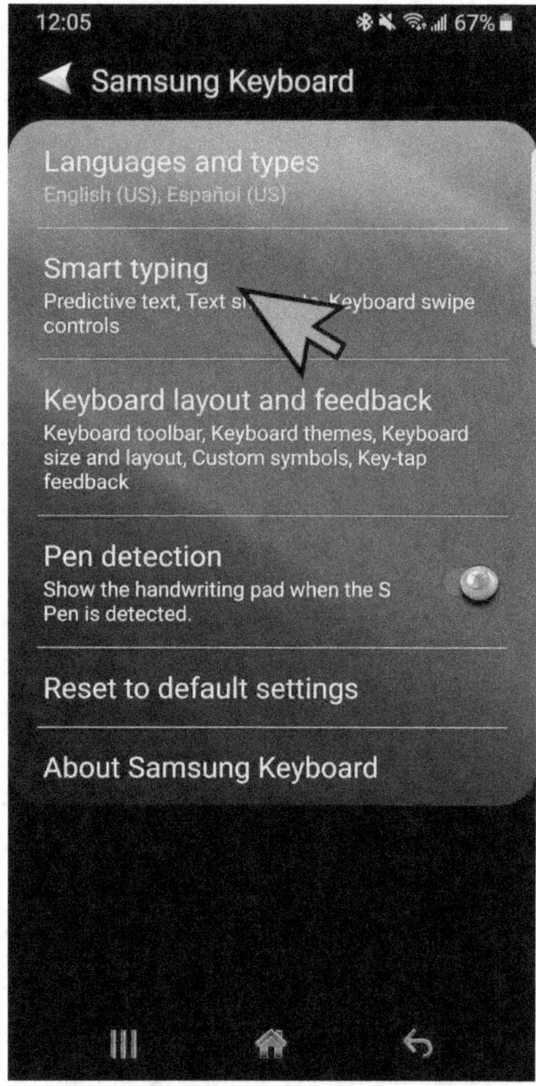

Tap on Smart Typing

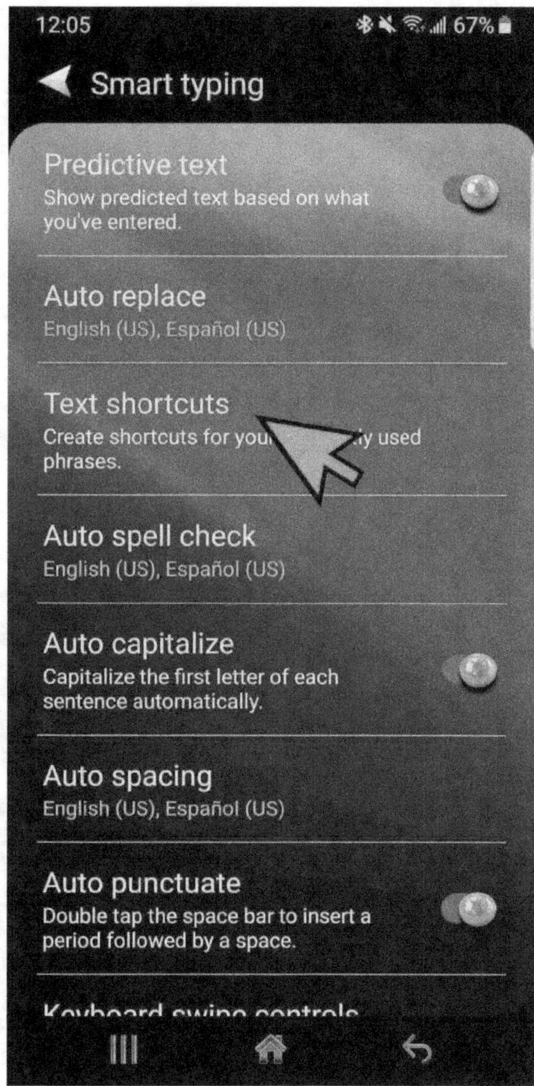

Tap on Text Shortcuts

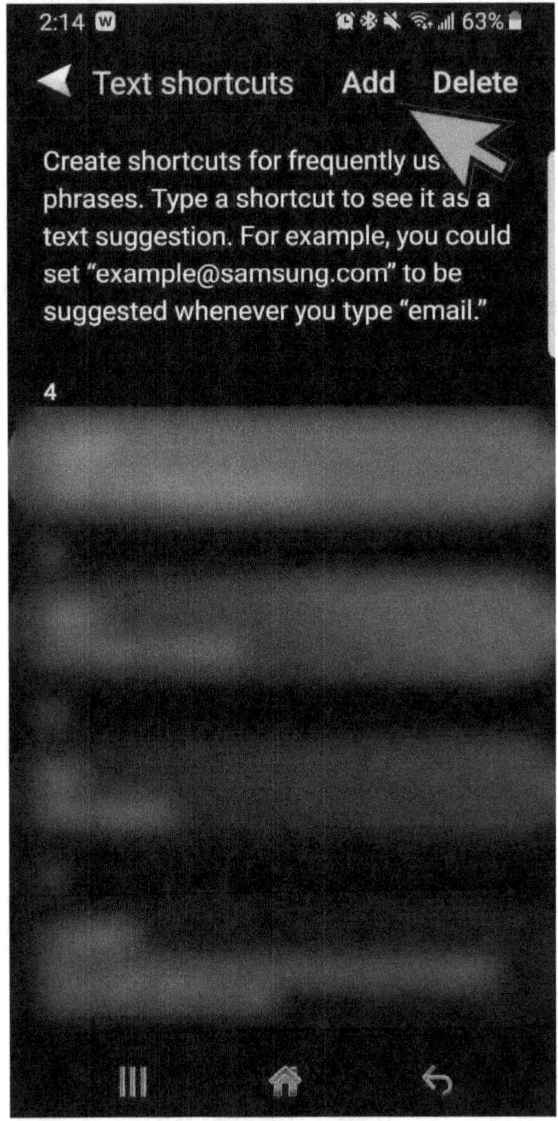

2:14
Text shortcuts   Add   Delete
Create shortcuts for frequently us
phrases. Type a shortcut to see it as a
text suggestion. For example, you could
set "example@samsung.com" to be
suggested whenever you type "email."
4

Tap on Add

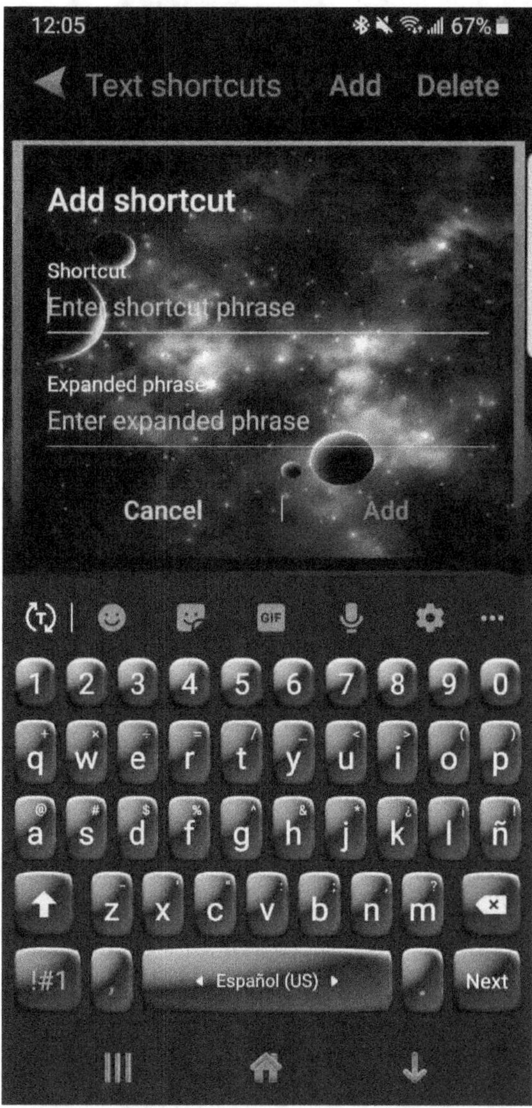

Type your shortcut and expanded phrase

Android (alternate, quicker method)

Tap on any text field to open the keyboard, then click on the Gear icon

You will be taken to the screen, where you can tap on Smart Typing and continue the rest of the steps from there.

10

The Best Text Expansion Apps

Selecting a text expander comes down to personal preference. There are many free and paid options, each with pros and cons.

Here are some of the most popular text expanding options.

aText

(https://www.trankynam.com/atext/)

I have been using aText for Mac for many years, and I believe its ease of use, features-set and price point ($4.99 per year or $29.99 for lifetime use) make it an excellent choice.

Among other features, aText allows you to create Rich-Text expansions that can include formatting options (Bold, Italic, Underline, etc.) as well as emojis and even pictures.

Pros:

- aText doesn't just let you add text to abbreviations, but also images and multimedia content.

- You can put your abbreviations into groups and subgroups.

Cons:

- The interface is a bit complicated and might take a little getting used to.

- Some users have experienced interruptions where they have to restart the app for it to work.

- If you want access to all of the features of aText, you'll need to download the paid version.

TextExpander

(https://textexpander.com)

This is one of the most popular text expanders, but it's not free. It includes a ton of features, like macros, team functions, etc.

Pros:

- Easy to use.

- Saves a HUGE amount of time.

- No impact on system performance.

- Extra handy features for coders.

Cons:

- Some may object to a subscription pricing model.

Magical

(https://chrome.google.com/webstore/detail/magicaltext-expander-aut/iibninhmiggehlcdolcilmhacighjamp?hl=en)

Pros:

- Magical's UI is simple and easy to learn.

- It uses JSON format, which allows you to import and export shortcuts.

Cons:

- Doesn't work on all websites (e.g. Google Docs)

- The features are pretty limited and basic – no dynamic fields except for date and time.

Text Blaze

(https://blaze.today)

Pros:

- Text Blaze has a 5-star rating on the Chrome Webstore, is trusted by over 100,000 users.

- It's free... forever.

- You can easily import snippets from other apps.

- You can create form fields to fill in with names or other data to personalize the message.

- Dynamic formulas mean you can calculate values when using the snippet.

- Text Blaze allows you to collaborate with other members of your team on shared snippets.

- Text Blaze works wherever you are in your Chrome browser, whether it's Gmail, Google Docs, Office 365, Salesforce, LinkedIn or any other site you use for work.

- You can use many of its unique features and get immediate value upon creating an account, all without a subscription.

Cons:

- Text Blaze is a Google Chrome extension, so it only works when using Chrome or Chromium-based browsers (e.g., Microsoft Edge).

Phrase Express

(https://www.phraseexpress.com)

Pros:

- PhraseExpress allows you to use dynamic phrases, as well as date and time stamps, to personalize your messages.

- You can share snippets with other members of your team.

- It works across multiple platforms.

Cons:

- If you want to access all the features that PhraseExpress offers, you'll need to sign up for the paid version.

- The PhraseExpress UI is not as user-friendly as other applications.

Other apps worth checking out

KeySmith

(https://www.keysmith.app/)

Expanso

(https://www.expanso.org/)

FastKeys

(https://www.fastkeysautomation.com/)

Mac's Native Text Replacement

If you own a Mac, you already have a fairly useful type of text expander. And it's free!

While macOS's built-in text replacement is adequate for most casual users, it falls short of the needs of professionals.

For example, certain writers working in fast-paced environments want hundreds of combinations at their fingertips. But macOS's built-in solution isn't ideal for those types of users. It requires going to Preferences to make changes, which is inefficient.

To use it, go to:

1. System Preferences

2. Keyboard

3. Text

4. Click the "+" sign

5. Add the shortcut in the "Replace" column

6. Add the expanded text in the "With" column

Conclusion

In summary, text expansion tools offer endless possibilities and can save you a lot of time.

However, having a text expander as part of your daily routine does more than simply save you time when typing repetitive words or phrases. It also makes you more aware of productivity speed bumps.

It is my hope that you found this book to be extremely valuable.

I appreciate you purchasing it.

Thank you so much, it means a lot to me.

Robert Moutal